TONY STEWART:
Instant Superstar!

BY MICHAEL TEITELBAUM

TRADITION BOOKS™
EXCELSIOR, MINNESOTA

Published by **Tradition Books**™ and distributed to the
school and library market by **The Child's World**®
P.O. Box 326
Chanhassen, MN 55317-0326
800/599-READ
http://www.childsworld.com

Photo Credits
Cover and title page: Sports Gallery/Brian Cleary (left): AP/Wide
  World (right)
Allsport: 19 (Amy Conn); 20 (Rusty Jarret); 21 (Vince Laforet); 26
  (Robert Laberge/GI)
AP/Wide World: 8, 14, 17, 18, 23
John Mahoney: 9, 11
Sports Gallery: 5, 6, 13, 15, 28, 30 (Brian Spurlock); 24 (Joe Robbins)

Book production by Shoreline Publishing Group, LLC
Art direction and design by The Design Lab

Library of Congress Cataloging-in-Publication Data
Teitelbaum, Michael.
  Tony Stewart, instant superstar! / by Michael Teitelbaum.
    p. cm. — (The world of NASCAR series)
Summary: A biography of Tony Stewart, whose Winston Cup rookie year of 1999 was the best
ever by a first-year driver in more than thirty years and set a NASCAR record. Includes biblio-
graphical references and index.
  ISBN 1-59187-011-9 (lib bdg. : alk. paper)
  1. Stewart, Tony, 1971– —Juvenile literature. 2. Automobile racing drivers—United States—
Biography—Juvenile literature. [1. Stewart, Tony, 1971– 2. Automobile racing drivers. 3.
NASCAR (Association)] I. Title. II. Series.
  GV1032.S743 T45 2002
  796.72'092—dc21   2002004650

Printed in the United States of America.

T O N Y   S T E W A R T

Table of Contents

INTRODUCTION

A Fast Start

E very so often a great, young NASCAR driver bursts onto the scene. He captures the imaginations of fans, the press, and his fellow drivers. When Tony Stewart showed up in 1999, he instantly grabbed everyone's attention.

Tony Stewart's Winston Cup **rookie** year of 1999 was the best by a first-year driver in more than 30 years. Winston Cup is the highest level in **NASCAR.** Tony finished his first year with three victories, the most ever by a rookie driver. When the 1999 season ended, Tony found himself in fourth place in the driver championship standings. He became the first rookie to finish in the top five in more than 30 years. He finished in fifth place or better in twelve races. This broke the rookie record set by the late Dale Earnhardt in 1979.

Former National Football League (NFL) coach Joe Gibbs

owns the car Tony drives. Gibbs knew that this young driver was good, but he didn't realize just how good. "None of us dreamed he'd win a race in his first year, much less win three!" Gibbs said. "None of us dreamed he'd finish in the top ten, much less the top five!"

Tony's success is no surprise to those who have known him for a long time. Racing has been his passion since childhood. His intense desire to compete and win fuels his progress as a driver. Tony's intensity is not without its drawbacks. Trouble has swirled around the young star in a number of races. Several times, he lost his temper and had arguments with other drivers.

With each year, however, he has matured as a person and

Handsome Tony Stewart is one of the most successful young drivers in NASCAR.

as a driver. Tony's second year in Winston Cup competition
saw him double his victory total. This fiery, dedicated young
driver rose to the top quickly. Now he plans to stay there for
a long time.

Tony's bright orange number 20 car is sponsored by
the Home Depot and many other companies.

CHAPTER ONE

Go-Karts, Midgets, Sprints, and Silver Crowns

Not every eight-year-old knows exactly what he wants to be when he grows up. Even fewer begin developing the skills needed to achieve that dream at such a young age. Only a special few go on to actually succeed at reaching that childhood goal in adult life. Tony Stewart was one of those special few.

He was born on May 20, 1971, in Rushville, Indiana. Tony showed an interest in race cars at a young age. When he was eight, Tony's mother introduced him to the world of **go-karts.** Go-karts are small, motorized vehicles. They don't

have much more than a frame and an engine. They're very low to the ground and easy for young drivers to operate. Tony soon spent time after school and on weekends racing. When he raced, he often won.

At the age of 12 in 1983, Tony won the International Karting Foundation Grand National Championship. It would be the first of many victories in cars of all sizes, shapes, and speeds. In 1987, Tony captured the World Karting Association national championship.

By the time Tony reached high school, he had moved up to midget cars. These are **open-wheel** cars that are minia- ture versions of big-time Indy cars. His passion for racing and

Tony raced go-karts like these, with smaller engines and wheels than regular cars, when he was a kid.

winning grew with each spin around the track. Soon, racing became the most important part of Tony's life. He made few friends in high school. Instead, he spent all his free time at the race track.

Success came for Tony at the midget-car level, too. The United States Auto Club (USAC) organizes three series of races on oval dirt tracks. Most young drivers begin with midget cars, as Tony did. They then move on to the larger sprint series. The highest USAC level is in Silver Crown cars, the most powerful USAC vehicles.

In 1989, Tony raced midgets on the USAC circuit. He won an award from racing fans as the best first-year driver. In 1991,

After go-karts, Tony moved up to the dirt-churning
excitement of midgets (above) and sprint cars.

he was voted the USAC Sprint Car Rookie of the Year. The following year, at the age of 21, Tony began racing full-time in the USAC, in all three series.

Soon, Tony was competing in USAC races all over the Midwest. Sometimes he drove in three or four races, in different states, all in the same weekend. In 1994, he was the national midget champion.

The 1995 season brought Tony the USAC's triple crown. He became the first driver to win championships in all three divisions in the same year. Only one driver, Pancho Carter, had won all three titles during a career. No other driver, however, had ever won all three in the same year. More people in the racing world began to take notice of this brash, fearless young man.

At this point in his career, Tony had to choose what his next step would be. He could try for the world of NASCAR stock racing. He also could move up to the next level of open-wheeled cars, called "Indy cars." Having grown up in Indiana, Tony

dreamed of one day racing in the world-famous Indianapolis 500 race. His choice for his next car was Indy cars. Tony Stewart was about to take his next big step up the ladder of racing success. He would let nothing stand in his way.

A NATION OF WHEELS

Tony Stewart often raced in events put on by the United States Auto Club. The USAC was founded in 1955 to organize racing in different cars at many levels. Today, the group puts on races in all parts of the country for both pro and ama-teur drivers. The races are for midget cars, stock cars, and other vehicles. Most races are held on smaller tracks at shorter distances than NASCAR races. Just as Tony did, many drivers "graduate" from USAC events to NASCAR.

The USAC is based in Indianapolis, Indiana. Until 1997, the group was responsible for organizing the Indy 500. Visit the USAC web site (see page 31) to learn more about this important motor sports organization.

Future NASCAR star Tony celebrates becoming the first driver to win the USAC "triple crown" in 1995.

C H A P T E R   T W O

Another Kind of Racing

n 1995, a new racing organization was created. The Indy Racing League (IRL) grew out of the classic Indy 500 race. Tony Stewart, the sport's top young driver, joined the IRL in 1996. His success helped the group became well-known.

Because he joined the IRL, Tony drove in the Indy 500. He finished second in a race at Walt Disney World, the first held by the IRL. For the Indy 500, Tony qualified for the **pole position.** He led the world-famous race for 44 **laps** and was named the race's top rookie.

The IRL staged only three races that year. That wasn't nearly enough to keep race-crazy Tony busy. So, although he had moved up a level, he still raced at all levels of USAC events. He also took his first step into the world of NASCAR stock car racing.

NASCAR's top-level races are part of the Winston Cup Series. One level below these are the competitions known as the Busch Grand National Series. Tony Stewart took part in nine Busch series races in 1996. In these, he got his first taste of stock car racing.

In 1997, Tony won the IRL series championship, finishing fifth in the Indy 500. That same year he also competed in five Busch races. He didn't win any of those NASCAR races. However, he did team up with the man with whom he would achieve his greatest success.

Joe Gibbs had been the head coach of the NFL's Washington Redskins. He had led them to three Super Bowl titles.

Tony made the "big time" in 1996 when he joined the
Indy Racing League, driving this open-wheeled car.

Gibbs then took his coaching skills to the world of stock cars as an owner of a NASCAR team. Top driver Bobby Labonte drove for Gibbs' Winston Cup team. Gibbs, however, was always on the lookout for bright young talent. The young and talented Tony Stewart quickly caught his eye.

In 1998, Tony raced full time in the IRL. He also drove in 22 Busch races for Joe Gibbs that year. Tony was gaining confidence and ability driving stock cars, and his relationship with Gibbs was growing stronger.

The stage was set. It was time for Gibbs to bring Tony Stewart up to the "big leagues." In 1999, Tony would explode onto the biggest of all stock car stages.

Race team owner Joe Gibbs, here with 2000 champ Bobby Labonte, saw a great future for Tony Stewart.

TONY STEWART'S RECORD BEFORE NASCAR

NASCAR BUSCH SERIES

Year	Races	Wins	Top 5	Top 10	Poles	Earnings	Ranking
1996	9	0	0	0		$45,140	49
1997	5	0	1	2	0	$48,625	57
1998	22	0	5	5	2	$270,820	21

INDY RACING LEAGUE YEAR-BY-YEAR

Year	Races	Wins	Top 5	Top 10	Poles	Earnings
1996	5	0	1	1	0	$422,303
1997	8	1	4	5	4	$1,017,450
1998	11	2	5	6	4	$1,002,850
1999	1	0	0	1	0	$186,670
2000	1	0	0	1	0	$218,850

Tony's success in the Busch Series in his number 44 car helped him make the jump to Winston Cup.

C H A P T E R   T H R E E

A Rookie to Remember

The move from the Busch series to the Winston Cup Series was a huge step for Tony in every way. To begin with, Winston Cup cars are larger and heavier than Busch cars. The level of competition increased dramatically, too.

Tony would now be going up against the best drivers in the world. His challengers included drivers such as eventual four-time champion Jeff Gordon and seven-time champion Dale Earnhardt. Even Bobby Labonte, Tony's teammate on Gibbs team, would prove a tough rival.

Tony's rookie year of 1999 kicked off as the NASCAR season always does—at the Daytona 500. From his first **qualifying laps,** Tony showed the big boys that he meant business. Tony started the 1999 Daytona 500 in the number two position. In the race itself, however, Tony finished 28th.

With his first Winston Cup performance under his belt, Tony was ready for more.

During Tony's next few races, he continued to improve steadily. He was gaining confidence in himself and earned respect from his fellow drivers. Among his early successes were a pair of sixth-place finishes in Darlington, South Carolina, and Texas.

Not everything went smoothly for Tony that first year. In July, at the Jiffy Lube 300 in Loudon, New Hampshire, Tony was well on his way to victory. Then, with just two laps

Tony made a splash as a rookie, starting in the number two position (bottom left) at the 1999 Daytona 500.

remaining, Tony was about to run out of gas. Knowing he couldn't finish without refueling, he pulled in for a **pit stop.** By the time he returned to the track, he had lost the lead and ended up finishing tenth.

An angry Tony stormed from the track, refusing to talk to reporters. The press called the young driver immature and arrogant. His reputation for being a "hothead" spread. Tony did not respond well to the criticism. "I am what I am," he told a reporter. "Take me or leave me."

Tony's first Winston Cup victory came late in the season at

In another show of temper, Tony fired some racing gear at Kenny Irwin's car after the two crashed.

a race in Richmond, Virginia. He dominated the race from the outset, leading for 333 of the race's 400 laps. Perfect **pit** stops late in the race clinched the victory over Bobby Labonte. Tony became the first rookie to win a Winston Cup race in more than a decade.

"They're all special," Tony later said about his victories. "But when you win in the Winston Cup series, you beat the best."

Tony won back-to back races in Phoenix and Miami late in the year. That brought his victory total to three, a NASCAR rookie record. When Tony's remarkable rookie year ended, he was fourth among all drivers in points. He also racked up 1,223 total laps, second only to Jeff Gordon. Tony earned more than twice as much money as any rookie in NASCAR history.

Tony's victory at Miami in late 1999 helped him set a rookie record for race victories.

It had been a great year, a record-setting one. Despite these achievements, however, the best was yet to come for Tony Stewart.

Tony's car gasses up during the Coca-Cola 600 in 1999. The race was run at night on a busy day for Tony.

DOING DOUBLE DUTY

On May 30, 1999, Tony Stewart drove in both the Indy 500 and the Coca-Cola 600. He drove a remarkable total of 1,090 miles (1,817 kilometers) in a single day.

His day began at 9:30 A.M. The Indy 500 got underway shortly before noon. After more than three hours of racing, Tony finished ninth. The race ended at 3:15 P.M. He took a quick shower and was checked by the track doctor. The doctor cleared him to drive in the second race that night.

A golf cart brought him to a helicopter, which rushed him to a nearby airport. A private jet took Tony to the North Carolina, landing about 4:45 P.M. Another helicopter shuttled him to the Lowe's Motor Speedway. At 6:15 P.M., Tony took off in the Coca-Cola 600, starting from the 43rd, or last, position.

After 80 laps, he began to feel weak and tired. He pressed on, despite his continuing fatigue and dehydration. Tony finished in fourth place. Climbing from his car, Tony's legs buckled as a medical team rushed to his aid. After some rest and lots of water Tony was okay.

He was proud that he had driven in both races, becoming the first man ever to do so. He had completed more miles in one day than any other driver in racing history. However, he decided that NASCAR would be his future. One race per day was plenty!

Tony steers his car in the Indy 500, the first of two long races he would run on one day in 1999.

C H A P T E R F O U R

Driver for a New Millennium

ony Stewart's 1999 debut season was terrific. The first season of the new millennium in 2000, however, brought him to new heights. He got off to a slow start and was in 13th place in points after nine races. Tony's hard work and persistence kept him moving forward. He also got some advice from teammate Bobby Labonte, who would win the series title in 2000.

"I know that I've got Bobby on my side," Tony explained. "He's only a phone call away or he's right there in the garage. Knowing that he's always close by and has the experience is a big help."

Tony was also realistic. It was helpful to have a talented

teammate. Once the race begins, however, each driver succeeds

or fails by himself. "If it comes down to me and Bobby for the

championship one year, then it's every man for himself," Tony

Way to go! Tony splashes teammate Bobby Labonte
after Labonte clinched the 2000 Winston Cup title.

pointed out. "However, I can't think of a better situation than to race Bobby for the championship. It would be great for our team. We could keep it in the family that way."

Tony soon posted back-to-back victories in Delaware and Michigan. He added another victory in a 300-mile (482-kilometer) race in New Hampshire. It was only July, and Tony had already equaled his win total for the previous year. There was now little question that Tony Stewart was a rising star.

Tony flashes across the finish line in Michigan, one of six victories he posted in 2000.

Following three top-10 finishes, Tony picked up his fourth and fifth wins of the 2000 season, winning again in Delaware and then in Virginia. Toward the end of the season, Tony won in Miami for the second straight year. His victory total of six was twice as many as in his first season. He finished sixth overall and broke Dale Earnhardt's record for most wins by a sophomore driver. Tony finished in the top five twelve times, and in the top ten 23 times. Tony Stewart was a NASCAR star to stay.

The 2001 season opened with great optimism. "It's great for me having Bobby close by, with him having won last year," Tony said as the 2001 season began. "But if I'm going to win a championship, I've got to have the same kind of consistency that Bobby had last year."

Tony won three more races in the 2001 season. Overall, Tony finished the 2001 season with 15 top-five finishes and 22 top-ten finishes. He finished second behind Jeff Gordon. It was Stewart's highest-ever finish in the all-important points race.

Nobody knows just how far this spectacularly talented

Tony continued his success in 2002, winning an early-season race in Atlanta.

driver will climb as a racer. His first Winston Cup season championship remains a key goal. Tony has been driving since he was eight years old. He has driven just about every kind of car there is. He has won at every level he has competed at. Now, making his NASCAR championship dream come true might just be the next step on his long, fast road.

STEWART'S NASCAR WINSTON CUP VICTORIES

Win #	Date	Race	Start*	Laps	Winnings
1	9/11/99	Exide Select Batteries 400	2	400	$135,160
2	11/7/99	Checker Auto Parts/Dura Lube 500	11	312	$168,485
3	11/14/99	Pennzoil 400 by Kmart	4	267	$278,265
4	6/4/00	MBNA Platinum 400	16	400	$152,830
5	6/11/00	Kmart 400	28	194	$123,800
6	7/9/00	thatlook.com 300	6	273	$164,800
7	9/24/00	MBNA.com 400	27	400	$158,535
8	10/1/00	NAPA AutoCare 500	1	500	$125,875
9	11/12/00	Pennzoil 400	13	267	$291,325
10	5/5/01	Pontiac Excitement 400	7	400	$150,175
11	6/24/01	Dodge/Save Mart 350	3	112	$139,875
12	8/25/01	Sharpie 500	18	500	$189,415
13	3/10/02	MBNA America 500	9	325	$174,978
14	5/5/02	Pontiac Excitement 400	3	400	$185,653

(*The position in which Tony started the race.)

With a combination of skill, good looks, and a great car,
Tony Stewart looks ahead to a bright future in racing.

TONY STEWART'S LIFE

1971 Born on May 20 in Indiana

1979 Drives his first race car, a go-kart

1983 Wins the International Karting Foundation Grand National Championship

1989 Starts racing midgets and sprint cars in the United States Auto Club

1995 Wins the United States Auto Club triple crown, taking the midget, sprint, and Silver Crown class championships all in the same year

1996 Starts racing in the Indy Racing League and the NASCAR Busch Grand National Series

1997 Joins Joe Gibbs' racing team

1999 Rookie year in the NASCAR Winston Cup Series; sets a record with three wins in his first year

2000 Doubles victory total from the previous year, winning six races

2001 Finishes second in the overall Winston Cup driver standings, his highest finish to date

GLOSSARY

amateur—an athlete who is not paid for his or her performance

dehydration—the loss of bodily fluids because of overwork or too much exercise or heat

go-karts—smaller, gas-powered vehicles, built very low to the ground

laps—a complete circuit around a track

NASCAR—National Association for Stock Car Automobile Racing

open-wheel—this refers to race cars without fenders

pit—the area just off the track where drivers go to have their car serviced during a race

pit stop—when racers leave the track and go to a special area called "pit road" where team members fuel the car and replace tires

pole position—first position when beginning a race

qualifying laps—to finish within the top group of racers during a preliminary race in order to enter the main race

rookie—an athlete in his or her first season in a sport

speedway—a paved track designed specifically for high-speed auto racing, containing seating for many spectators

Racing is a team sport. That's most true during action-filled pit stops like this one.

FOR MORE INFORMATION ABOUT TONY STEWART

Books

Mello, Tara Barkus. *Tony Stewart*. Broomall, Penn.: Chelsea House Publishers, 2001.

Utter, Jum. *Tony Stewart: Hottest Thing on Wheels*. Champaign, Ill.: Sports Publishing, Inc., 2001.

Web Sites

Tony Stewart's Official Web Site
http://www.tonystewart.com
Stewart's official site contains more biographical information and details on his fan club.

The Official Web Site of NASCAR
http://www.nascar.com
For an overview of an entire season of NASCAR as well as the history of the sport and a dictionary of racing terms

The United States Auto Club
http://www.usaracing.com
The official web site of the United States Auto Club tells fans where and how they can see the many races sponsored by the organization.

INDEX

ABOUT THE AUTHOR

Michael Teitelbaum has been a writer and editor of children's books and magazines for more than 20 years. He was editor of *Little League Magazine for Kids,* the author of a two-volume encyclopedia on the Baseball Hall of Fame, and the writer/project editor of *Breaking Barriers: In Sports, In Life,* a character education program, based on the life of Jackie Robinson. Teitelbaum's most recent book is *Great Moments in Women's Sports.*